Syllables and Affixes, Volume 2

Words Their Way

CLASSROOM

SAVVAS
LEARNING COMPANY

SAVVAS Learning Company LLC, 15 East Midland Avenue, Paramus, NJ 07652

Cover Anneka/Shutterstock; ARTIKAL/Shutterstock; Janis Abolins/Shutterstock; Mathee Suwannarak/Shutterstock; Perunika/Shutterstock

ISBN 13: 978-1-4284-4192-7
ISBN-10: 1-4284-4192-1
6 20

Contents

Unaccented Final Syllable -le

cradle	middle	tremble
able	table	single
settle	bottle	scribble
rifle	muscle	sample
rattle	paddle	battle
bugle	bridle	handle
cable	jungle	scramble

Unaccented Final Syllable -le

VCle	VCCle doublet	VCCle
title	**little**	**simple**

1. Read each sentence. Choose a word from the box that best completes the sentence and write it on the line. (Note: Not all words have to be used and each word can be used only once.)
2. Draw a line between the two syllables in each word.
3. Underline the accented syllable of each word.

scramble	battle	cable	rattle	scribble	able	rifle
handle	tremble	settle	cradle	bugle	jungle	single
table	paddle	bridle	middle	muscle	sample	bottle

1. The kayaker used her ____________________ to glide across the water.
2. Amin's family eats dinner at the ____________________ each night.
3. Megan's hands ____________________ when she is nervous.
4. The audience heard the ____________________ blare at the concert.
5. The athlete pulled a ____________________ while running.
6. The veterinarian used his hands to ____________________ the kitten.
7. Sonya ordered a ____________________ of water with lunch.
8. Monkeys and tigers live in the ____________________.
9. The rock climber used a safety ____________________ when climbing.

Unaccented Final Syllable /əl/ Spelled -le, -el, -il, -al

saddle	level	April
total	fragile	couple
angel	fossil	metal
special	angle	novel
evil	signal	needle
pedal	stencil	local
bundle	vowel	journal
cancel	pupil	jewel
struggle	council	

Unaccented Final Syllable /əl/ Spelled -le, -el, -il, -al

-le	-el	-il	-al	Oddball
cattle	model	pencil	final	

1. Write on the lines words that contain -le, -el, -il, or -al in the final syllable.
2. Underline the accented syllable of each word.

-le	-el	-il	-al	Oddball
cattle	model	pencil	final	

Unaccented Final Syllable /ər/ Spelled -er, -ar, -or

Sort 31

brother	doctor	dollar
favor	rather	solar
cover	flavor	mirror
motor	sugar	grammar
weather	silver	father
rumor	polar	tractor
mother	harbor	lunar
nectar	cedar	after
cellar	flower	error

-er	-ar	-or
spider	**collar**	**color**

1. Write on the lines words that contain -er, -ar, or -or in the final syllable.
2. Draw a line between the two syllables and underline the accented syllable in each word.
3. Choose three words and use each in a sentence. Write your sentences on the lines below.

-er	-ar	-or
spi/der	col/lar	col/or

1. ______________________________

2. ______________________________

3. ______________________________

dreamer	creator	longer
faster	driver	sailor
stronger	farmer	visitor
smaller	jogger	editor
fresher	writer	younger
swimmer	older	smoother
voter	director	juror
governor	shopper	brighter

Agents and Comparatives

People Who Do Things		Words to Compare
dancer	**actor**	**bigger**

1. Read each word. Make new words by adding the ending *-er* or *-or*. (Double the final consonant and drop the *e* as necessary.) Write the new words on the lines.
2. Write an A above the agents and a C above the comparatives.

Agent or Comparative		Agent or Comparative	
shop	______	edit	______
old	______	write	______
dream	______	strong	______
create	______	young	______
big	______	vote	______
drive	______	smooth	______
visit	______	sail	______
fast	______	farm	______
jog	______	govern	______
fresh	______	swim	______
dance	______	small	______
direct	______	act	______
bright	______	jury	______

Final Syllable /ər/ Spelled -cher, -ture, -sure, -ure

rancher	nature	pressure
failure	senior	teacher
capture	pleasure	danger
pitcher	future	leisure
mixture	treasure	pasture
culture	posture	obscure
secure	stretcher	marcher

Final Syllable /ər/ Spelled -cher, -ture, -sure, -ure

-cher = /chur/	-ture = /chur/	-sure = /zhur/	-ure = /yur/	Oddball
catcher	**picture**	**measure**	**figure**	

Write on the lines words that contain *-cher*, *-ture*, *-sure*, or *-ure* in the final syllable.

-cher = /chur/	-ture = /chur/
catcher	**picture**

-sure = /zhur/	-ure = /yur/	Oddball
measure	figure	

Unaccented Final Syllable /ən/ Spelled -en, -on, -an, -ain

Sort 34

-en	-on	-an	-ain	Oddball
broken	**dragon**	**human**	**mountain**	
eleven	curtain	bargain	pardon	apron
woman	bacon	ribbon	captain	hidden
gallon	urban	chosen	stolen	certain
heaven	cotton	slogan	organ	villain
orphan	mission	children	fountain	

Unaccented Final Syllable /ən/ Spelled -en, -on, -an, -ain

-en	-on	-an	-ain	Oddball
broken	dragon	human	mountain	

1. Read the beginning of each word. Choose the final syllable -en, -on, -an, or -ain that best completes the word.
2. Write the new word on the line and read it aloud.
3. Choose three words and use each in a sentence. Write your sentences on the lines below.

elev___ __________	fount___ __________
cott___ __________	heav___ __________
capt___ __________	ribb___ __________
wom___ __________	chos___ __________
stol___ __________	orph___ __________
gall___ __________	apr___ __________
barg___ __________	curt___ __________
org___ __________	slog___ __________
hidd___ __________	childr___ __________
urb___ __________	bac___ __________
vill___ __________	pard___ __________
	cert___ __________

1. ____________________

2. ____________________

3. ____________________

Unaccented Final Syllable /ət/ Spelled -et, -it, -ate

Sort 35

-et	-it	-ate	Oddballs
jacket	**edit**	**climate**	
bandit	comet	credit	habit
magnet	orbit	pirate	planet
ballet	private	quiet	racket
limit	rocket	senate	summit
target	unit	buffet	visit
secret			

Unaccented Final Syllable /ət/ Spelled -et, -it, -ate

-et	-it	-ate	Oddballs
jacket	edit	climate	

1. Write on the lines words that end with -et, -it, or -ate.
2. Underline the accented syllable of each word.
3. Choose three words and use each in a sentence. Write your sentences on the lines below.

-et	-it	-ate
jacket	edit	climate

1. ______________________________

2. ______________________________

3. ______________________________

Final -y, -ey, and -ie

Sort 36

-ey	-ie	y = /ē/	y = /ī/
money	**cookie**	**very**	**July**
body	brownie	candy	volley
cherry	deny	dizzy	donkey
eerie	goalie	journey	berry
monkey	movie	pinkie	reply
story	turkey	twenty	valley

Final -y, -ey, and -ie

-ey	-ie	y = /ē/	y = /ī/
money	**cookie**	**very**	**July**

Read each of the words in the box. Write each word in the correct column.

body	volley	goalie	donkey	cherry	deny	dizzy	eerie	movie	valley
journey	berry	monkey	turkey	pinkie	reply	twenty	brownie	candy	

-ey	-ie	y = /ē/	y = /ī/
money	cookie	very	July

another	degree	believe
divide	awhile	depend
between	direct	among
desire	beneath	upon
aboard	develop	because
against	defend	begun
afraid	aloud	astonish
behavior	agenda	decision
beforehand	delete	

Unaccented Initial Syllables a-, de-, be-

a-	de-	be-	Oddball
again	**debate**	**beyond**	

1. Read the ending of each word. Choose the initial syllable a-, de-, or be- that best completes the word.
2. Write the new word on the line and read it aloud.
3. Choose two words and use each in a sentence. Write your sentences on the lines below.

___nother ______	___neath ______
___gree ______	___board ______
___lieve ______	___velop ______
___stonish ______	___cause ______
___while ______	___gainst ______
___yond ______	___fend ______
___pend ______	___gun ______
___tween ______	___bate ______
___mong ______	___fraid ______
___sire ______	___loud ______
___gain ______	___lete ______
___genda ______	___havior ______
___forehand ______	___cision ______

1. ______________________________________

____

2. ______________________________________

____

Initial Hard and Soft c and g

Sort 38

Soft c	Soft g	Hard c	Hard g
cement	**gentle**	**correct**	**gather**
circle	collect	general	cent
gossip	gurgle	cider	garage
camel	gymnast	cereal	custom
genius	central	cavern	gingerbread
cyclist	golden	common	govern
gutter	college	giraffe	giant

Initial Hard and Soft c and g

Soft c	Soft g	Hard c	Hard g
cement	gentle	correct	gather

1. Read each sentence. Choose a word from the box that best completes the sentence and write it on the line. (Note: Not all words will be used and each word can be used only once.)
2. Underline the vowel that follows the c or g.
3. Circle the word if it has a soft c or g.

circle	central	cent	cyclist	cider	gather
gymnast	giraffe	genius	govern	giant	correct
common	cavern	college	custom	collect	cement
gossip	golden	garage	gutter	cereal	gentle

1. The book club will ____________________ weekly.
2. The ____________________ gained speed on the downhill slope.
3. Aida plans to major in biology at ____________________.
4. The teacher outlined the ____________________ concept of the project.
5. The craftsman made a ____________________ desk.
6. My cousin is training to become a ____________________.
7. Apple ____________________ was served at the harvest party.
8. Some of the leaves had changed to a ____________________ color.
9. Malik volunteered to ____________________ the problem.
10. There was a ____________________ breeze near the ocean.
11. The class measured the diameter of the ____________________.
12. Cheryl stores her athletic equipment in the ____________________.
13. We explored the underground ____________________.
14. Our teacher asked for a volunteer to ____________________ our reports.
15. My teacher discourages ____________________ at school.

Final -s and Soft c and g

fidget	manage	police	garbage
actress	sentence	gadget	princess
distance	surgeon	address	luggage
office	compass	package	science
village	practice	message	courage
arrange	challenge	possess	express

Final -s and Soft c and g

-ce = /s/	-ss = /s/	ge = /j/	-age = /ij/
notice	recess	budget	bandage

Write on the lines words that contain -ce, -ss, ge, or -age in the final syllable.

-ce = /s/	-ss = /s/	-ge = /j/	-age = /ij/
notice	recess	budget	bandage

More Words With g

Sort 40

vague	guard	language
gauge	shrug	league
guitar	zigzag	guide
fatigue	iceberg	argue
strong	guilty	guest
dialogue	guidance	plague
intrigue	catalog	penguin

More Words With g

gu-	-gue	-g	Oddball
guess	vogue	ladybug	

Read each sentence. Choose a word from the box that best completes the sentence and write it on the line. (Note: Not all words will be used and each word can be used only once.)

guard	guitar	guide	guilty	guidance
vague	league	fatigue	strong	plague
zigzag	shrug	iceberg	guest	intrigue
gauge	language	argue	dialogue	catalog

1. The musician played a ____________ while she sang.
2. My grandfather has a ____________ memory of his childhood.
3. Claire picked out a new outfit from the ____________.
4. The coach encouraged the players to ____________ off their loss.
5. Jin planned his class schedule with some ____________ from his advisor.
6. The smell of the fresh flowers was ____________.
7. The bowling ____________ competes on Saturday mornings.
8. Tourists followed a tour ____________ around the city.
9. My grandmother speaks more than one ____________.
10. The actor memorized his ____________ for the movie.
11. After the marathon, Marcella was overcome with ____________.
12. The hikers followed the ____________ path down the mountain.
13. We went to the auditorium to hear the ____________ speaker.
14. The penguins gathered on the ____________.
15. A light went on when the gas ____________ was near empty.

/k/ Spelled ck, -ic, -x

Sort 41

quick	pocket	traffic
index	stomach	hammock
nickel	topic	complex
attack	pickle	picnic
buckle	metric	ticket
electric	plastic	perplex
shoebox	jacket	racetrack
rocket	fabric	unlock
struck	specific	

/k/ Spelled ck, -ic, -x

-ck	ck	-ic	-x	Oddball
shock	chicken	magic	relax	

Write on the lines words that contain the /k/ sound spelled as ck, -ic, or -x.

-ck	ck	-ic
shock	chicken	magic

-x	Oddball
relax	

/kw/ and /k/ Spelled qu

quality	frequent	racquet	squirrel
equipment	mosquito	squirming	equator
conquer	quadrant	banquet	quotation
inquire	quizzes	liquid	queasy
sequence	sequel	request	qualify
technique	critique		

1st Syllable	2nd Syllable	qu = /k/
question	equal	antique

1. Read each sentence. Choose a word from the box that best completes the sentence and write it on the line. (Note: Not all words will be used and each word can be used only once.)
2. Draw a line between the syllables in each word.

request	quality	sequel	conquer	inquire	queasy
question	frequent	mosquito	equator	quizzes	sequence
equal	racquet	squirming	banquet	liquid	qualify
antique	equipment	squirrel	quotation	technique	quadrant

1. The tennis player prepared to serve by raising his ________________.
2. Snowstorms in the northeast are ________________ in winter.
3. Shayna located the ________________ on the globe.
4. My grandmother has several ________________ quilts in her home.
5. Some of the kids felt ________________ after the roller-coaster ride.
6. My sister hopes to ________________ for the race.
7. The coach spoke at the awards ________________.
8. The ________________ buried the acorns in the yard.
9. Luckily, I returned from the forest with no ________________ bites.
10. My backpack is made of ________________ material.
11. The team hoped to ________________ its opponent.
12. The hiker was responsible for carrying her ________________ on the expedition.
13. Raj called the radio station with his music ________________.
14. Our English teacher likes to give surprise ________________.
15. Vonelle could not wait to read the ________________ to the novel.

fasten	resign	wreckage
knowledge	honor	thought
listen	assignment	wrestle
rhyme	brought	glisten
answer	rhythm	bought
khaki	though	doorknob
campaign	kneepad	soften
gnarl	sword	knockout

Silent t	Silent g	Silent w
castle	design	wrinkle

Silent k	Silent h	Silent gh
knuckle	honest	through

1. Read the incomplete word. Choose the silent letter t, g, w, k, h, or letters gh that best completes the word.
2. Write the new word on the line and read it aloud.
3. Choose three words and use each in a sentence. Write your sentences on the lines below.

fas___en ______________	r___ythm ______________
___nowledge ______________	thou___ ______________
lis___en ______________	___neepad ______________
r___yme ______________	s___ord ______________
ans___er ______________	___reckage ______________
campai___n ______________	thou___t ______________
___narl ______________	___restle ______________
k___aki ______________	glis___en ______________
resi___n ______________	bou___t ______________
___onor ______________	door___nob ______________
assi___nment ______________	sof___en ______________
brou___t ______________	___nockout ______________

1. ____

____

2. ____

____

3. ____

____

physics	elephant	cough
naughty	phantom	nephew
tough	taught	photocopy
dolphin	rough	caught
photograph	trophy	laughter
fought	telephone	homophone
paragraph	phonics	height

Words With gh and ph

ph-	ph	-gh = /f/	Silent gh
phrase	alphabet	enough	daughter

1. Write words on the lines that contain ph, gh = /f/, and silent gh.
2. Choose three words and use each in a sentence. Write your sentences on the lines below.

ph-	ph	-gh = /f/	silent gh
phrase	alphabet	enough	daughter

1.

2.

3.

recopy	uncle	unkind
recycle	unwrap	reptile
refill	unselfish	refinish
unbutton	unhappy	rewrite
retrace	unpack	retake
unfair	return	uneven
review	unequal	unbeaten
remodel	rescue	

Prefixes re-, un-

re-		un-		Oddball
rebuild		unable		

1. Write the meaning of the prefix on the line next to each header.

Prefix re-: ____________________

Prefix un-: ____________________

2. Make new words by adding the prefix re- or un- to the following base words. Write the words on the lines. (Note: You can add more than one prefix to some words.)

___build ____________	___button ____________
___able ____________	___write ____________
___copy ____________	___trace ____________
___cycle ____________	___pack ____________
___kind ____________	___take ____________
___wrap ____________	___fair ____________
___fill ____________	___turn ____________
___selfish ____________	___even ____________
___finish ____________	___view ____________
___happy ____________	___equal ____________
___model ____________	___beaten ____________

dislike	mistreat	prefix
precious	disable	mismatch
premature	disobey	misplace
preteen	displace	misbehave
preview	dishonest	misjudge
preheat	disloyal	pretest
disappear	precaution	mister
miscount	distant	mistrust

Prefixes dis-, mis-, pre-

dis-	mis-	pre-	Oddball
disagree	misspell	preschool	

1. Make new words by adding the prefix dis-, mis-, or pre- to the following base words. Write the words on the lines. (Note: You can add more than one prefix to some words.)

___like ________________	___behave ________________
___treat ________________	___view ________________
___fix ________________	___honest ________________
___able ________________	___judge ________________
___match ________________	___heat ________________
___mature ________________	___loyal ________________
___obey ________________	___test ________________
___place ________________	___appear ________________
___teen ________________	___caution ________________
___cover ________________	___agree ________________
___spell ________________	___school ________________
___count ________________	___trust ________________

2. Choose three derived words and write a definition for each.

1. ____
2. ____
3. ____

Prefixes ex-, non-, in-, fore-

Sort 47

ex-	non-	in- ("not")	in- ("in" or "into")	fore-
exclude	**nonsense**	**incomplete**	**indent**	**forecast**
extend	foremost	forehead	inhuman	income
forearm	insight	foresee	incorrect	nonprofit
indecent	nonskid	explode	nonstop	indoor
exhale	nonfiction	expand	express	nonfat
foreshadow	exit	explore		

Prefixes ex-, non-, in-, fore-

ex-	non-	in- ("not")	fore-
exclude	**nonsense**	**incomplete**	**forecast**
		in- ("in" or "into")	
		indent	

1. *Write the meaning of the prefix on the line next to each header.*

Prefix ex-: ______________________

Prefix non-: ______________________

Prefix in-: ______________________

Prefix fore-: ______________________

2. *Make new words by adding the prefix ex-, non-, in-, or fore- to the following base words or word parts. Write the words on the lines. (Note: You can add more than one prefix to some words.)*

___tend	________	___shadow	________
___fiction	________	___plode	________
___correct	________	___come	________
___arm	________	___most	________
___plore	________	___pand	________
___stop	________	___door	________
___decent	________	___sight	________
___head	________	___human	________
___press	________	___complete	________
___fat	________	___sense	________
___see	________	___cast	________
___clude	________	___dent	________
___profit	________	___skid	________

Prefixes uni-, bi-, tri-, and Other Numbers

trilogy	biweekly	unity	unique
unicorn	triangle	bisect	octagon
pentagon	bilingual	triple	octopus
union	triplet	October	unison
tripod	uniform	trio	universe

Prefixes uni-, bi-, tri-, and Other Numbers

uni-	bi-	tri-	Other Number Prefix
unicycle	**bicycle**	**tricycle**	**quadrangle**

1. Write the meaning of the prefix on the line next to each header.

Prefix uni-: ______________________

Prefix bi-: ______________________

Prefix tri-: ______________________

Other Number Prefix: ______________________

2. Make new words by adding the prefix uni-, bi-, tri-, or that of some other number to the following base words or word parts. Write the words on the lines. (Note: You can add more than one prefix to some words or word parts.)

___cycle	______	___lingual	______
___rangle	______	___ple	______
___ty	______	___opus	______
___weekly	______	___on	______
___logy	______	___plet	______
___agon	______	___ober	______
___corn	______	___son	______
___sect	______	___pod	______
___angle	______	___form	______
___que	______	___verse	______

Suffixes -y, -ly, -ily

clearly	quickly	easily
angrily	rainy	foggy
snowy	noisily	lazily
loudly	quietly	dimly
stormy	misty	windy
daily	cloudy	roughly
chilly	sleepily	breezy
busily	smoothly	merrily

-y	-ly	-ily
sunny	**slowly**	**happily**

1. Read each sentence. Choose a base word from the box that best completes the sentence. (Note: Not all words will be used and each word can be used only once.)
2. Add the suffix -y, -ly, or -ily to the word. (Change -y to i, drop the e, and double the final letter as necessary.) Write the adjective or adverb on the line.

rain	clear	lazy	storm	cloud	breeze	merry
quick	angry	mist	loud	rough	happy	sleepy
easy	snow	quiet	chill	wind	sun	busy
fog	dim	noisy	day	smooth	slow	

1. During ________________ weather, we prepare to stay indoors.
2. The emergency vehicle moved ________________ to the hospital.
3. After much practice, Dana ________________ completed the equation.
4. We used a flashlight to explore the ________________ lit cave.
5. My family likes to ski in a ________________ location.
6. Our cat ________________ moved from the floor after napping.
7. The news anchor ________________ delivered his lines.
8. Greg ________________ shared his good news with the class.
9. At the library, we work together ________________.
10. The excited friends ________________ greeted one another.
11. Flying a kite is fun to do on a ________________ day.
12. Talia shielded her face from the ________________ wind.
13. The parade of people passed ________________ through town.
14. The hikers moved ________________ up the steep path.
15. On ________________ days it's fun to look for shapes in the sky.

calmer	prettiest	dirtier
easiest	closer	crazier
coolest	calmest	hotter
fewest	closest	craziest
weaker	prettier	easier
dirtiest	fewer	hottest
cooler	weakest	lazier
funniest	laziest	funnier

Comparatives -er, -est

-er	-est	-ier	-iest
braver	**bravest**	**happier**	**happiest**

1. Make new words by adding the comparative ending -er and -est to the following base words. (Change -y to i, drop the e, and double the final letter as necessary.) Write the words on the lines.
2. Write three new base words on the lines provided. Make new words by adding the comparative ending -er and -est to these words. (Change -y to i, drop the e, and double the final letter as necessary.) Write the words on the lines.

	-er	-est
funny	__________	__________
lazy	__________	__________
calm	__________	__________
easy	__________	__________
close	__________	__________
pretty	__________	__________
few	__________	__________
crazy	__________	__________
cool	__________	__________
dirty	__________	__________
hot	__________	__________
weak	__________	__________
brave	__________	__________
happy	__________	__________
__________	__________	__________
__________	__________	__________
__________	__________	__________

Suffixes -ness, -ful, -less

colorful	goodness	hopeless	thankfulness
thoughtfulness	faithful	happiness	helplessness
illness	weakness	restless	peacefulness
kindness	painful	penniless	worthless
fearful	harmless	dreadful	plentiful
truthfulness	awareness	gratefulness	fearless

Suffixes -ness, -ful, -less

-ness	-ful	-less	Combination of Suffixes
darkness	**graceful**	**homeless**	**carelessness**

1. Write the meaning of the suffix on the line next to each header.

Suffix -ness: ______________________________

Suffix -ful: ______________________________

Suffix -less: ______________________________

2. Make new words by adding the suffix -ness, -ful, or -less, or a combination of these suffixes to the following base words. (Change -y to i as necessary.) Write the words on the lines.

care	______	ill	______
home	______	thought	______
dark	______	rest	______
grace	______	peace	______
good	______	kind	______
color	______	hope	______
hope	______	pain	______
thank	______	penny	______
weak	______	happy	______
faith	______	fear	______
worth	______	harm	______
help	______	plenty	______
dread	______	truth	______
aware	______	grate	______

cellar	weather
allowed	flour
bored	seller
whether	aloud
flower	board
vary	their
desert	principle
chews	merry
very	higher
dessert	principal
choose	marry
there	hire

berry	bury

1. Say each word aloud. Think of a word that sounds the same but is spelled differently and has a different meaning.
2. Write a sentence that uses the new word.
3. Underline the homophone.

cellar ______________________________

weather ______________________________

allowed ______________________________

flower ______________________________

board ______________________________

their ______________________________

merry ______________________________

very ______________________________

dessert ______________________________

principal ______________________________

choose ______________________________

hire ______________________________

bury ______________________________

desert ______________________________

aloud ______________________________

Homographs

noun		verb	
present		pre**sent**	
desert	rec**ord**	per**mit**	re**bel**
permit	de**sert**	**rec**ord	**reb**el
sub**ject**	**ob**ject	**re**ject	ob**ject**
subject	**pro**duce	con**duct**	**ex**port
conduct	re**ject**	pro**duce**	con**tract**
ex**port**	**con**tract		

noun		verb	
present		pre**sent**	

Write a sentence using each word as a noun and a verb.

present ______________________________

desert ______________________________

record ______________________________

permit ______________________________

rebel ______________________________

object ______________________________

subject ______________________________

reject ______________________________

produce ______________________________

conduct ______________________________

export ______________________________

contract ______________________________

i Before e Except After c

ie = /ē/	cei = /ē/	ei = /ē/	ei = /ā/
thief	**receive**	**seize**	**neighbor**
grief	sleigh	belief	field
ceiling	conceit	deceive	reign
eighteen	either	freight	neither
weigh	niece	protein	receipt
relieve	retrieve	shield	yield

i Before e Except After c

ie = /ē/	cei = /ē/	ei = /ē/	ei = /ā/
thief	**receive**	**seize**	**neighbor**

Write on the lines words with long *e* and long *a* spelled *ie* or *ei*.

ie = /ē/	cei = /ē/	ei = /ē/	ei = /ā/
thief	receive	seize	neighbor